MY AMERICAN STORY

MAKING THE RULES

WHAT DOES OUR GOVERNMENT DO?

DK | Penguin Random House

Editorial Management by Oriel Square
Produced for DK by Collaborate Agency
Index by James Helling

Author Jehan Jones Radgowski
Series Editor Megan DuVarney Forbes
Publisher Nick Hunter
Publisher Sarah Forbes
Publishing Project Manager Katherine Neep
Production Controller Isabell Schart
Picture Researcher Nunhoih Guite
Production Editor Shanker Prasad

First American Edition, 2023
Published in the United States by DK Publishing
1745 Broadway, 20th Floor, New York, NY 10019

A catalog record for this book
is available from the Library of Congress.
ISBN 978-0-7440-7766-7

DK books are available at special discounts when purchased
in bulk for sales promotions, premiums, fund-raising, or educational use.
For details, contact: DK Publishing Special Markets,
1745 Broadway, 20th Floor, New York, NY 10019
SpecialSales@dk.com

Printed and bound in China

For the curious
www.dk.com

CONTENTS

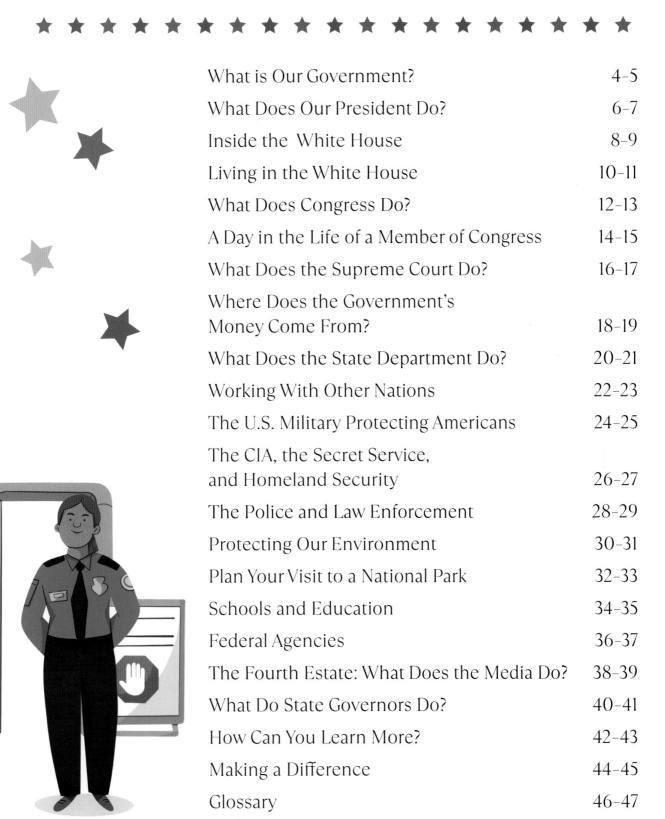

WHAT IS OUR GOVERNMENT?

★ ★ ★ ★ ★ ★ ★ ★ ★ ★ ★ ★ ★ ★ ★ ★ ★ ★ ★

THE CONSTITUTION

You live in a **community**. The community is in a town or a city, which is in a county. The county is in a state. The state is part of the United States of America. As citizens of the United States, you and your family get to make decisions, such as which state you live in. Who makes the decisions for the entire country? Why do these people get to make those choices?

A government is a system of rules and the people who make and enforce these rules. Cities, counties, and states have governments, too. In the U.S., our federal government is a **democratic** republic. It is a republic because it is run by elected officials. It is democratic because these officials are voted into office by the citizens. The people chosen by Americans to run the country are called **representatives**. Most countries have some type of democratic government, although there are many countries where citizens do not choose the government. Some countries are **monarchies**, ruled by a king or queen.

The U.S. was built on the idea that three different groups or branches should share control of the government. This is called separation of powers. The Executive Branch includes the president and members of their **cabinet**. The Legislative Branch, or Congress, makes the laws. The **Judicial** Branch, or the federal courts and judges, interprets the laws.

How do those jobs get filled and what do all these people do?

DID YOU KNOW?

ALMOST 250 YEARS AGO, THE AMERICAN COLONIES THAT BECAME THE U.S. WERE RULED BY KING GEORGE III OF GREAT BRITAIN. THE COLONIES DECLARED THEIR **INDEPENDENCE** FROM GREAT BRITAIN IN 1776.

THE BALD EAGLE IS A SYMBOL OF THE UNITED STATES.

WHAT DOES OUR PRESIDENT DO?

★ ★

The president is the leader of the U.S. In 1789, George Washington became the first U.S. president. Before he became president, George Washington led the colonial military against the British in the American Revolution. The American Revolution happened between 1775 and 1783.

Joe Biden was sworn in as the 46th president on January 20, 2021. Presidents are almost always inaugurated on January 20. Large crowds gather in Washington, D.C. to watch the inauguration ceremony and millions watch it on TV.

The president's main job is to enforce the laws of the U.S. That is no easy task.

The president listens to information and advice from people in all parts of the **federal** government. Then the president makes decisions. He or she is also the Commander-in-Chief of the U.S. military. That means the president makes decisions about military action.

THE WASHINGTON MONUMENT REMEMBERS THE FIRST PRESIDENT.

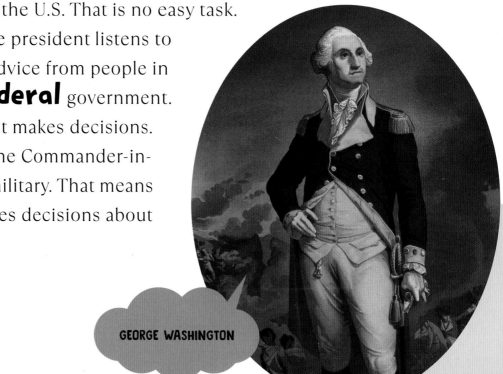

GEORGE WASHINGTON

HOW OFTEN IS A NEW PRESIDENT ELECTED? ★

JOE BIDEN

A president is elected every four years. The president can win a re-election campaign only once. This means that each president can only serve up to eight years in total. During each year of the presidency, the president has a constitutional responsibility to deliver the State of the Union Address, a speech given each year that explains what is currently happening in the country.

Each candidate for president picks their vice president before the election. Biden chose Kamala Harris. Harris became the first female vice president of the U.S. She is also the first woman of color to become vice president.

INSIDE THE WHITE HOUSE

★ ★

The White House has 132 rooms and about 90 people work there. The president and his or her family live in the White House residence. This is a short walk from the **Oval Office**.

The president works at his or her desk in the Oval Office in the **West Wing** of the White House. The Press Room, the Situation Room, and other meeting rooms are also in the West Wing.

In the Press Room, the press secretary meets with journalists every day to answer questions. The First Amendment to the Constitution guarantees freedom of the press. This means that journalists can write or say whatever they like about the president. For example, they can write or say if they think he or she is doing a good job or not.

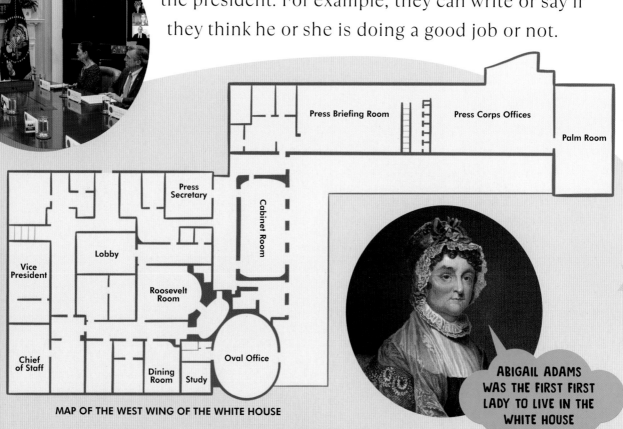

Press Briefing Room

Press Corps Offices

Palm Room

Press Secretary

Cabinet Room

Lobby

Vice President

Roosevelt Room

Chief of Staff

Dining Room

Study

Oval Office

MAP OF THE WEST WING OF THE WHITE HOUSE

ABIGAIL ADAMS WAS THE FIRST FIRST LADY TO LIVE IN THE WHITE HOUSE

DID YOU KNOW?

THE WHITE HOUSE ALSO HAS A BOWLING ALLEY, A THEATER, AND AN OUTDOOR POOL. AN INDOOR POOL WAS BUILT IN 1933. IN 1970, PRESIDENT NIXON PUT THE PRESS ROOM ABOVE THE POOL. THE POOL IS STILL BURIED UNDER THE FLOOR.

The president receives secret briefings in the **Situation Room**. There is also a soundproof room for making private phone calls. Key members of the military and government representatives work in the Situation Room.

White House workers say every day is different. Sometimes they have four to five events at the house each day. For example, the president might have breakfast with a visiting foreign leader. After a few phone calls, the president might meet the winner of the National Spelling Bee. Later that night, the president could host an awards ceremony for soldiers who defended the country.

LIVING IN THE
WHITE HOUSE

★ ★

When your parent is the president, you grow up in the White House. Chelsea Clinton, Jenna and Barbara Bush, and then Malia and Sasha Obama were all recent White House daughters. In 2017, **Baron Trump** became the first boy to grow up in the White House since John F. Kennedy Jr. in the 1960s.

BARON TRUMP

In some ways, White House children have normal lives. They go to school and they have homework. They have friends and they have sleepovers. However, they sometimes run into celebrities or world leaders in their home, and Secret Service agents follow them everywhere, even to school.

RESCUE CAT. WILLOW BIDEN. MOVED INTO THE WHITE HOUSE WITH PRESIDENT JOE BIDEN.

Many presidents brought their pets to live in the White House with them. President Barack Obama had two **Portuguese Water Dogs** named Bo and Sunny. Some presidents have had horses, lizards, and even a cow.

★ WHITE HOUSE ★ CELEBRATIONS

One tradition at the White House is the **celebration** of holidays. Almost every spring the White House hosts the Easter Egg Roll. It started in 1878 when children came to the White House and asked President Rutherford B. Hayes if they could enter and play Easter games. Ever since, there has been some sort of celebration. Often children whose parents are in the military are invited to the Easter event. Other holidays such as Christmas, Hanukkah, Thanksgiving, and the Fourth of July are also celebrated at the White House.

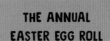

THE ANNUAL EASTER EGG ROLL

WHAT DOES CONGRESS DO?

★ ★

The **legislature** includes both houses of Congress: the Senate and the House of Representatives. Senators and Members of the House of Representatives are elected by citizens. The legislature creates new laws, such as laws to collect new taxes. In addition to making laws, the approval of Congress is needed for nearly every decision that is made about running the country. There are few things the president can do without this approval.

★ HELPING PEOPLE ★ WITH DISABILITIES

Congress creates laws so that the country runs smoothly and citizens are treated fairly. Plans to change the law start with citizens speaking out. Concerned citizens can meet with their Congressional representatives and demand change.

For example, in the past, there were no laws to ensure people with disabilities could use public transportation and bathrooms, or access places like schools and parks. They were also treated unfairly when they applied for jobs. Citizens argued that all Americans should have the same rights.

In 1973, Congress passed a law giving people with disabilities the same opportunities to work for the government as others. In 1990, it passed the Americans with Disabilities Act (ADA). The ADA ensured equal treatment of people with disabilities in all areas.

★ FROM CUBA ★ TO WASHINGTON

When Lleana Ros-Lehtinen was young, her family fled Cuba and came to the U.S. as refugees. A **refugee** is a person who leaves their home country to find safety in another country. Lleana became a teacher. There were things she wanted to change about education, so she went into politics. In 1986, she became the first Cuban-American in the Senate and the first Hispanic woman as well. She worked to change laws about the environment, international politics, and human rights.

LLEANA ROS-LEHTINEN REPRESENTED FLORIDA'S 27TH CONGRESSIONAL DISTRICT FROM 1989 TO 2019.

A DAY IN THE LIFE OF A MEMBER OF
CONGRESS

★ ★ ★ ★ ★ ★ ★ ★ ★ ★ ★ ★ ★ ★ ★ ★ ★ ★ ★ ★

Imagine you're a member of Congress. What's your day like?

8:00 am   Meet staffers. Staff do research and help the Congressperson make decisions.

9:00 am   Coffee with a colleague. You wrote a bill, but you need to make sure it has support. You will also find out what your colleague is working on. Maybe they have a bill you can support?

10:00 am

Present your bill to the Congress. Some members don't like your bill, but you need to convince them that it is important.

12:00 pm   A quick walk and a sandwich. After lunch, you read your emails.

2:00 pm

Return to the Chamber to vote on a bill.

3:00 pm

A video call with students from your home state. They want you to protect local wetlands. A company wants to build

a shopping mall near the wetlands. You want more jobs for your hometown, but the students make a good point. The wetland is home to birds and insects. You have to protect it!

4:00 pm

Play in a friendly Congressional basketball game.

6:00 pm   The game is over. Your team lost, but there's always next week. Time to go home and have dinner.

8:00 pm

You figure out how to save the wetlands and build the mall. You write up a bill to protect the wetlands. You ask the mall

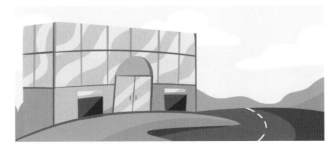

developer to build on an abandoned lot on the other side of town. Everyone is going to be happy.

10:00 pm   You're tired. Time for bed!

WHAT DOES THE SUPREME COURT DO?

★ ★ ★ ★ ★ ★ ★ ★ ★ ★ ★ ★ ★ ★ ★ ★ ★ ★ ★

The president runs the nation by enforcing the law. Congress creates the laws. The Supreme Court decides if the laws have been broken and what to do about it. It also makes decisions relating to the Constitution, which sets out the rules for how the U.S. is governed.

JUSTICES ARE CHOSEN BY THE PRESIDENT AND THEN APPROVED BY THE SENATE.

Members of the Supreme Court are called **justices**. There is one Chief Justice and eight Associate Justices.

The Supreme Court has made many decisions that have impacted many people's lives. They have also overturned decisions of past Supreme Courts. One of its most famous cases was Brown versus the Board of Education. In some states, Black and white children went to different schools and did not get an equal education. In 1954, the court said this was illegal. This ruling said that separating children by race was unconstitutional, or not allowed by the U.S. Constitution.

★ FREEDOM OF SPEECH ★

In 1969, three students were suspended from school because they wore black arm bands to protest the war in Vietnam. The school told the students to take off the arm bands or go home. The students said they had the right to freedom of speech and expression. Freedom of speech and expression means everyone has the right to say what they want or express themselves without getting in trouble. The Supreme Court said the students were right. Everyone has the right to freedom of speech, even when in school. However, the Court also said that this freedom only goes so far—students cannot disrupt the school day or make it hard for others to learn.

HONORABLE KETANJI BROWN JACKSON JOINED THE SUPREME COURT IN 2022

WHERE DOES THE GOVERNMENT'S MONEY COME FROM?

★ ★ ★ ★ ★ ★ ★ ★ ★ ★ ★ ★ ★ ★ ★ ★ ★ ★ ★ ★

The government needs money to pay for all its employees and programs. The **money** that the national government has to spend, comes from the federal budget. Money in the federal budget mostly comes from the taxes of individual people and businesses.

The Nineteenth **Amendment** to the Constitution gives the government permission to charge taxes on the money people earn. This means that, when you work, part of the money you make goes to the government. There are other taxes too, such as taxes on some goods when they are brought into the country. The government uses this money to pay for things that benefit us all. For example, this money is used to pay the military to protect the country.

THE FIRST INCOME TAX WAS INTRODUCED BY PRESIDENT ABRAHAM LINCOLN IN 1861

There is a big debate around taxes. Some people say that taxes are too high. Others say that taxes should be higher. Some think the money the government receives should be spent differently. Depending on where you live, **there can also be state and local government taxes to pay.**

REVOLUTION ★ AGAINST TAX ★

The American Revolution started because people in the American colonies didn't want to pay taxes to the British government. The difference in colonial times was that the British government wanted people in the American colonies to follow British rules and pay taxes, but not to have any say in their government. This was called taxation without representation. The colonists didn't like that and they fought back. First they refused to pay taxes and next they took up arms.

WHAT DOES THE
STATE DEPARTMENT DO?

★ ★

When the U.S. started its fight for independence from Great Britain, the new nation needed friends overseas. Building relations with other nations is called **diplomacy**. Benjamin Franklin is known as one of the Founding Fathers of the U.S. and for his scientific investigations. Did you know he was also the first American diplomat? In 1776, Franklin was sent to France to get French support for American independence. He urged the French to help the American colonists and give them supplies, money, and soldiers.

BENJAMIN FRANKLIN

★ U.S. ★
DIPLOMACY

The State Department sends diplomats appointed by the president to foreign countries. Diplomats work to improve relations between the U.S. and the country to which they have been appointed by serving as representatives of our country. One of their jobs is to advance U.S. business interests in other countries. They also help Americans who are in other countries and need help.

SPASO HOUSE IS THE MOSCOW HOME OF THE U.S. AMBASSADOR.

Diplomats work in U.S. consulates or embassies in the country to which they have been appointed. The Embassy is led by the **Ambassador**, or the Chief of Mission. Some Embassies are very large, while others are small. Diplomats are part of the Foreign Service. They live in a country for two to four years and then change to a new country. Some diplomats speak many languages. It's important for them to learn the customs of their host country, too.

CHILDREN OF DIPLOMATS USUALLY GROW UP OVERSEAS. THEY GO TO INTERNATIONAL OR LOCAL SCHOOLS.

Diplomats' children often learn the language of the country they are living in. The classes can be very different from in the U.S. In Russia, diplomat kids ice skate for P.E.

WORKING WITH
OTHER NATIONS

★ ★ ★ ★ ★ ★ ★ ★ ★ ★ ★ ★ ★ ★ ★ ★ ★ ★ ★ ★

The U.S. works one-on-one with other countries with the help of diplomats. It also works with other countries through international organizations like the United Nations.

★ WHAT IS THE UNITED NATIONS? ★

The United Nations, or UN, was formed in 1945 after World War II to help countries develop peaceful relationships with each other. The UN has 193 member countries. Its headquarters are in New York City.

The UN is a place where people from all countries can discuss the issues that face everyone, such as war and climate change. Leaders try to come up with solutions to the world's problems.

The UN recognizes certain world days. These days help to educate people and promote special causes. If the UN recognizes it, many countries follow.

Some examples include:

- World Water Day on March 22
- World Autism Awareness Day on April 2
- International Youth Day on August 12.

THE UN SECURITY COUNCIL

The U.S. also works with other countries through international agreements called treaties. The Senate approves these treaties and the State Department manages most treaties that the U.S. signs. Treaties are written on many different subjects like human rights, the environment, and trade.

DID YOU KNOW?

SOME SPORTS ARE ORGANIZED INTERNATIONALLY, TOO. THE SUMMER AND WINTER OLYMPIC GAMES BRING PEOPLE TOGETHER EVERY FOUR YEARS, ALONG WITH THE PARALYMPICS FOR ATHLETES WITH DISABILITIES. DID YOU KNOW THERE ARE ALSO THE OLYMPIC YOUTH GAMES? IN THE YOUTH GAMES, MORE THAN 200 COUNTRIES SEND THEIR BEST 15–18 YEAR OLDS TO COMPETE.

THE U.S. MILITARY
PROTECTING AMERICANS

★ ★ ★ ★ ★ ★ ★ ★ ★ ★ ★ ★ ★ ★ ★ ★ ★ ★ ★ ★

The military defends America. Sometimes the military also defends other countries which are America's partners. There are six branches of the U.S. military: the Army, Navy, Airforce, Marine Corps, Coast Guard, and Space Force. People volunteer to join the military.

WHAT DOES THE MILITARY DO?

Members of the military do many different jobs. They:

- help after a natural disaster by distributing food or medical aid

- stop pirates (yes, there are still pirates causing problems on the high seas!)

- help with law enforcement

- provide security at U.S. embassies abroad.

★ MILITARY ★ TRAINING

DID YOU KNOW?

THE ARMY IS THE OLDEST BRANCH OF THE MILITARY. THE U.S. ARMY WAS CREATED BEFORE THE U.S. ITSELF! THE ARMY SEAL ORIGINALLY SAID THE DEPARTMENT OF WAR. WE NO LONGER HAVE A DEPARTMENT OF WAR. NOW WE HAVE A DEPARTMENT OF DEFENSE.

When someone joins the military, they usually go to basic training. In basic training they prepare their minds and their bodies to be part of the military. They might have to carry heavy backpacks while running miles, learn how to use weapons, or climb buildings. No matter the service, basic training teaches teamwork.

Not everyone in the military goes into combat. There are also doctors, photographers, musicians, computer programmers, and scientists working in the military.

THE CIA,
THE SECRET SERVICE, AND HOMELAND SECURITY

★ THE CIA—CENTRAL INTELLIGENCE AGENCY ★

Can you keep a secret? A CIA agent can! When one of these agents finds out something about another person, business, or country that not everyone knows, it is known as intelligence, or intel. The CIA is a U.S. government **agency** that gathers the intel of other countries. They take that information, study it, and then provide it to the president and other American leaders, like Congress. The president uses the intel to make decisions.

★ THE SECRET SERVICE ★

Another agency that can keep a secret is the Secret Service. They protect the president, their family, and other leaders. They also protect leaders from other countries when they visit America. A little known fact is the Secret Service also protects America's money and financial system. If someone was creating fake U.S dollars, the Secret Service would find and stop them.

HOMELAND ★ SECURITY ★

On September 11, 2001, terrorists hijacked four airplanes that had taken off from American airports. The terrorists used the airplanes as weapons and flew them into the World Trade Center in New York and the Pentagon in Washington, D.C. The fourth airplane crashed in a field in Pennsylvania before reaching its intended target. These attacks killed many people and injured more.

In response to the 9/11 tragedy, President George W. Bush created the U.S. Department of Homeland Security (DHS). Its mission is to protect the U.S. from threats such as **terrorism.** DHS also strives to protect against natural disasters. It creates plans for extreme weather like tornadoes or earthquakes and gives training to prepare for natural disasters. DHS also assists Americans whose homes and businesses have been destroyed by disasters.

PRESIDENT
GEORGE W. BUSH

THE POLICE
AND LAW ENFORCEMENT

★ ★

★ THE FBI ★

Before 1908, there was no agency that could investigate crime. No one could track criminals as they moved from state to state, or stop someone from breaking laws in multiple states. The **Federal Bureau of Investigation** (FBI) was created in 1908 to be a national law enforcement agency and to protect Americans.

Everyday, FBI agents find criminals, prevent **cybercrimes**, stop other countries from finding out America's intel, and more. In some cases that involve multiple U.S. states, FBI agents might work closely with state police departments.

★ THE POLICE ★

The Police Departments enforce state and local governments' laws. Much of their funding comes from their local area. The first American police force was created in Boston in 1838. Businesses in Boston wanted someone to help protect them from theft.

Hundreds of years later, police still **enforce** state and local laws that help protect businesses, but they also help protect individuals. Police engage local communities to improve trust and fight crime.

Different Police departments are different sizes. New York Police Department (NYPD) has 50,000 employees but a small city police force might only have five police officers. Officers work together to investigate crime, handle traffic accidents, and respond to emergencies.

DID YOU KNOW?

SOME POLICE DEPARTMENTS HAVE A K-9 UNIT MADE UP OF SPECIALLY TRAINED DOGS AND THE OFFICERS THAT WORK WITH THEM. POLICE DOGS MIGHT SEARCH FOR MISSING CHILDREN, SEARCH A CRIME SCENE FOR MISSING CLUES, OR FIND OUT IF SOMEONE IS HIDING DRUGS OR **EXPLOSIVES**. IF YOU SEE A K-9 DOG, DON'T PET THEM. IF THEY ARE WORKING, THEY ARE TRYING HARD TO FOLLOW THEIR HANDLER'S COMMANDS.

PROTECTING
OUR ENVIRONMENT

★ ★

The U.S. has many different types of environments, from polar to tropical. The country has lakes, oceans, mountains, rainforests, farmlands, and cities. All of these areas need care and we need to make rules to make sure they are protected.

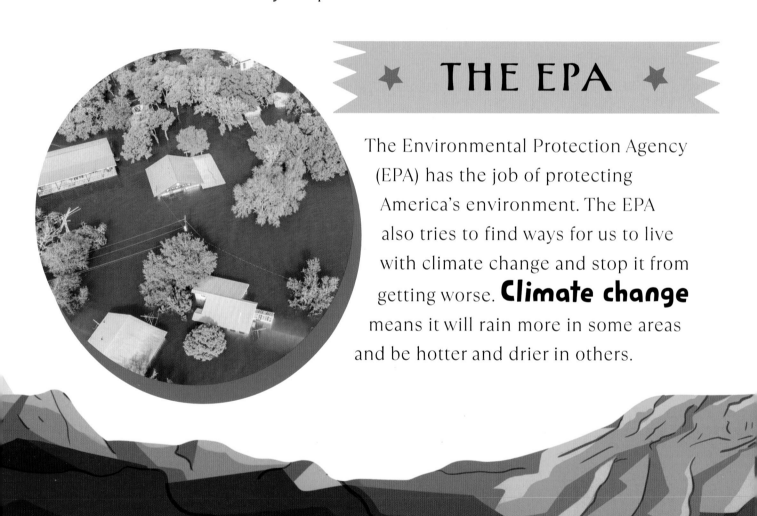

★ THE EPA ★

The Environmental Protection Agency (EPA) has the job of protecting America's environment. The EPA also tries to find ways for us to live with climate change and stop it from getting worse. **Climate change** means it will rain more in some areas and be hotter and drier in others.

YELLOWSTONE NATIONAL PARK. WYOMING

THE NPS

In 1872, Congress made the first National Park. It was Yellowstone in Wyoming. The vast and wild park has bears, bison, and many natural hot-water springs called **geysers**. People who care about the environment asked Congress to make more National Parks. In 1916, President Woodrow Wilson created the National Park Service (NPS). The NPS is part of the Department of the Interior. Today the NPS protects over 80 million acres of land in all 50 states. There are more than 400 parks.

WHAT DO PARK RANGERS DO?

The people who work at the NPS are park rangers. Park rangers have many jobs. Some say hello to visitors when they arrive. Others create programs for their park, so visitors can learn about America's amazing natural areas. Some protect their park from people who want to illegally cut down trees or hunt wildlife. Other rangers are ready to **help** people who get hurt.

PLAN YOUR VISIT TO A
NATIONAL PARK

★ ★ ★ ★ ★ ★ ★ ★ ★ ★ ★ ★ ★ ★ ★ ★ ★ ★ ★ ★

All National Parks are different. You might camp or stay in a lodge. Sometimes you can go for a swim or ski. For any National Park adventure, make a plan first.

★ STEP ONE ★

Figure out your budget to see how far you can travel. If you live in California, you're lucky! That is the state with the **most** national parks.

★ STEP TWO ★

What **adventure** do you want to have? If you want to hug a tree, check out Sequoia National Park. It has some of the world's biggest trees. Not scared of heights? Check out Grand Canyon National Park in Arizona. You can take a hike or ride your bike along the South Rim.

SEQUOIA NATIONAL PARK, CALIFORNIA

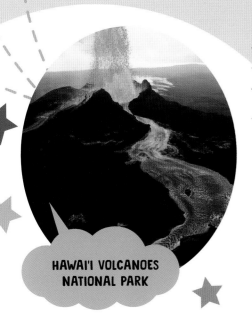

HAWAI'I VOLCANOES
NATIONAL PARK

★ STEP THREE ★

When will you travel? Are your activities weather dependent? Check out Acadia National Park in Maine for snow shoeing. For warm sunny days, check out Hawai'i Volcanoes park. Be careful—it has **active** volcanoes!

★ STEP FOUR ★

Check the NPS website www.nps.gov. It has park maps and **tips** on what to pack. You should find out if the park you are visiting has any restrictions or special events coming up.

★ STEP FIVE ★

Have fun! When you arrive, meet the rangers. Weather conditions or other issues may impact your trip. Follow the rangers' instructions, such as no selfies with the bears! Take your trash out of the park, but nothing else! Leave all the plants, stones, and seashells for the next person or animal to enjoy. National Parks are one of our greatest treasures.

Enjoy!

IF YOU CAN'T TRAVEL NOW, DON'T WORRY. MOST PARKS HAVE VIRTUAL TOURS AND OTHERS HAVE WEBCAMS HIDDEN ALL AROUND. CHECK OUT WWW.NPS.GOV FOR MORE INFORMATION.

SCHOOLS
AND EDUCATION

★ ★ ★ ★ ★ ★ ★ ★ ★ ★ ★ ★ ★ ★ ★ ★ ★ ★ ★ ★

The first leaders of the U.S. knew that the citizens of their new nation needed schools and education. **Education** would enable citizens to read and understand political issues and, once old enough, choose who to vote for. In the 1700s only a few children could go to private schools. By 1830, most states had a system of public schools, and half of all children were going to elementary school. Most, however, did not go on to high school at the time.

When the Constitution was written, education was not recognized as a right for all. However, the Tenth Amendment says any powers not given to the federal government by the Constitution are given to the States. Therefore, state and local governments have most control over education. They decide what is taught or not taught in a school. The Fourteenth Amendment to the Constitution says that states must treat all their citizens fairly. It is law in every state that children must attend school and the Department of Education, makes sure that all students are given equal rights while at school.

While school is usually provided for all, colleges are **private**. This means that students have to pay expensive tuition, or money to attend the college. The government helps some students with tuition by giving them a loan. Students use this loaned money to pay their college tuition, but must then pay it back to the government at a later date.

DID YOU KNOW?

EACH STATE SCHOOL SYSTEM CAN DECIDE OVERALL HOW THEIR SCHOOLS ARE RUN. SOME SCHOOLS HAVE P.E. EVERYDAY OR TEACH LOTS OF LANGUAGES. CHILDREN UNDER DIFFERENT SCHOOL SYSTEMS ALSO TAKE DIFFERENT EXAMS. THOUSANDS OF CHILDREN DON'T GO TO SCHOOL AT ALL, BUT DO THEIR LEARNING AT HOME.

FEDERAL
AGENCIES

★ ★

There are over 100 federal agencies which do important work for the government. Here are a few that you might find interesting!

★ CENSUS BUREAU ★

Every ten years, the Census Bureau counts every person who is living in the country. The U.S. Constitution says that every person must be counted. The information is used to decide how many representatives each state gets. It also helps the government make decisions like how many roads or schools need to be built.

THE NATIONAL ARCHIVES ★

The National Archives is called the nation's **record keeper**. It keeps documents created by the federal government. The Constitution is kept at the archives. It also has other documents like notes from presidents to foreign leaders. The archives will keep these documents safe forever.

SMITHSONIAN INSTITUTION

The Smithsonian is the world's largest collection of museums. It includes 19 museums and the National Zoo. In the National Museum of Natural History, you can walk through the Butterfly Pavilion where 300 butterflies live. At the National Museum of the American Indian, **you can see artifacts from over 12,000 years ago**.

SPACE COMMAND ★ (SPACECOM) ★

SpaceCom is responsible for ensuring that the U.S. is protected from any attack from space. They are mostly on the lookout for an enemy using satellites for weapons. SpaceCom should not be confused with the National Aeronautics and Space Administration (NASA). NASA is responsible for space exploration. NASA is currently working to get back to the Moon.

THE FOURTH ESTATE:
WHAT DOES THE MEDIA DO?

★ ★ ★ ★ ★ ★ ★ ★ ★ ★ ★ ★ ★ ★ ★ ★ ★

The **media** are often called the fourth estate. Media include newspapers, radio and T.V. stations, and the internet.

In a democracy, journalists help keep the government on track. They report on the activities of the government. They report when people are elected and when projects are completed. They also report bad news. They report when there is a case of fraud or when the government wastes money. For example, the government wastes millions of dollars every year on heating and maintaining their empty buildings that aren't in use.

The Constitution demands that Congress protect freedom of the press. It says,

"Congress shall make no law ...prohibiting...the freedom of speech, or of the press...."

In countries without freedom of the press, journalists are sometimes put in jail if they print a story that does not support their government.

THE
PHE
How Alex
Ocasio-C
became A
lightning r
BY CHARLOTTE
ALTER

CHANGING
THE CLIMATE
FIGHT
BY JUSTIN
WORLAND

★ WHAT IS ★ FAKE NEWS?

Fake news is when someone creates news that's wrong and spreads it to others. Some people make fake news because they do not like the truth. Others make fake news to try to convince people to change their minds on something. For example, if someone didn't want to brush their teeth, they could tell everyone that dentists now say that brushing your teeth is bad for your health.

Fake news is becoming more and more common, and is often spread on social media.

EVERYONE NEEDS TO CHECK THEIR SOURCES!

WHAT DO
STATE GOVERNORS DO?

★ ★ ★ ★ ★ ★ ★ ★ ★ ★ ★ ★ ★ ★ ★ ★ ★ ★ ★

Each of the 50 states has its own government. State governments are organized in a similar way to the federal government. States have judicial and legislative bodies. All states have agencies that work in areas like education and health. Many states collect taxes to provide services, such as schools and libraries, for their citizens.

Similarly to how the president leads the U.S., individual states are also run by a person who is elected by citizens. These people are called state governors. They approve the state budgets and laws. They can also request the help of the National Guard, which is a branch of the military that has both state and federal responsibilities. In emergency situations, the president also asks the National Guard for help.

Most governors live in big homes called mansions. The governor of New York's mansion once had a petting zoo with bears, monkeys, and other animals.

A governor's **term** is four years. Virginia is the only state that does not allow the governor to be elected for two terms in a row. The governor of Virginia can run again in the future but never right after they finish their first term. Many of the states do not have term limits. This means that a person could be re-elected as governor as many times as the people want.

NELLIE ROSS. THE FIRST WOMAN GOVERNOR OF WYOMING.

DID YOU KNOW?

THE U.S. FLAG HAS 13 STRIPES AND 50 STARS. THE 13 STRIPES REPRESENT EACH OF THE ORIGINAL COLONIES OF THE U.S. THE 50 STARS REPRESENT EACH U.S. STATE. THE NUMBER OF STARS COULD INCREASE, BUT THE NUMBER OF STRIPES NEVER WILL.

HOW CAN YOU LEARN MORE?

★ ★ ★ ★ ★ ★ ★ ★ ★ ★ ★ ★ ★ ★ ★ ★ ★ ★ ★ ★

One day, you may be an agent in the FBI or a diplomat solving world issues. Or maybe **you will be the president** of the U.S. However, you don't have to wait for the future to explore more about what our government can do.

You can visit the White House right now. Public tours are available on most days. All White House tours are free. While you are in Washington, D.C., have a picnic on the National Mall and visit one of the many Smithsonian museums.

POLLUTION IN YOUR LOCAL RIVER IS SOMETHING YOU MAY WANT TO WRITE TO YOUR MEMBER OF CONGRESS ABOUT.

If you can't travel to Washington, D.C., don't worry. You can do a lot without even leaving your home. First figure out who your members of Congress are. Your U.S. representative is based on your zip code. Your senator is based on your state. Figure out who they are and send them a letter. If there is something you are passionate about, tell them about it and describe the change you'd like to see. Or if you want to meet them, let them know.

You can do the same for your governor, mayor, or even school board representatives. These people all work for you. You should attend their public town hall meetings with your parents or another adult. You can see elected **officials** in action on T.V. Some officials have days when children can come to their meetings.

PROTECTING THE ENVIRONMENT IS A BIG ISSUE FOR MANY YOUNG PEOPLE.

MAKING A
DIFFERENCE

★ ★ ★ ★ ★ ★ ★ ★ ★ ★ ★ ★ ★ ★ ★ ★ ★ ★ ★

If you see something wrong in your community, stand up and say something. If the slide in your playground needs to be replaced, you can report that at a local town hall meeting. Or you can write a letter to your mayor letting him or her know. Several children and teens just like you have made a difference in their communities and, sometimes, across the world.

★ KID ★
GOVERNORS

What about kids who want to run for office right now? There's a program called Kid Governor® for 5th grade students created by The Connecticut Democracy Center and now operating in several states. In this program, the elected child gets to be the Kid Governor for one year. Connecticut's first Kid Governor, Elena Tipton, worked on promoting kindness and reducing bullying. She inspired 15 Connecticut schools and playgrounds to add Buddy Benches. A Buddy Bench is where a kid can go to find a friend. It's really helpful when you're sad and need to find nice people.

To run for Kid Governor, you must first check to see if your state participates. Then you pick your platform. The platform is the area you hope to focus on. For example, one of Oregon's Kid Governors, Emerie Martin, worked to prevent animal abuse. After you have chosen your platform, you explain it to other kid voters by creating a video. Students in the entire state will vote and the winner will be the governor!

GET THE ★ KNOWLEDGE ★

Whether you are planning to run for office now or in the future, or planning to write your letter to your Congressional representative, knowing how your government is organized is the first step to success.

Know your Constitutional rights and how your government works!

GLOSSARY

agency
an organization set up by government to manage a particular area or subject

ambassador
an official sent by one country to live in another country and represent their home country

amendment
a change or addition to a legal document, such as a constitution

artifacts
objects made by humans in the past that can tell us about history or culture

bill
a proposed law debated in Congress

cabinet
the heads of executive agencies who advise a president and carry out their plans

chamber
a large room where lawmakers meet to debate bills

climate change
changes to Earth's climate, which most scientists believe is caused by human activity

colleague
a fellow worker or official

cybercrimes
crimes committed online, such as spreading computer viruses or stealing money by accessing someone's bank account

democracy
a political system in which the government is chosen by citizens voting in an election

executive
referring to the branch of government that carries out and enforces laws

federal
the name for the U.S. national government or any government with powers shared between states and a national government

independence
when a country becomes free from the control of another country's government

judicial
referring to the court system in a government

justice
a judge in the Supreme Court

legislature
the part of a government that makes laws, which is made up of the Senate and the House of Representatives in the U.S.

media
a collective name for ways of communicating, such as TV, newspapers, and the Internet

official
someone who works for the government or another public organization

refugee
a person who leaves their home country to find safety in another country

representatives
people who are chosen to represent a group of people, such as elected members of Congress

tax
money paid to the government to be used for public services

term
the length of time an elected official holds their job for

terrorism
threats or violence against people, carried out for political reasons

INDEX